MY WELLBEING WORKBOOK

THE MELANATED WOMAN'S RESOURCE TO SELF-DISCOVERY, EMBRACING SELF-CARE, AND CREATING AN INTENTIONAL LIFE.

ROSE-STELLA PIERRE-LOUIS

© 2021 Rose-Stella Pierre-Louis

All rights reserved. No part of this publication may be reproduced, distributed, or transmitted in any form or by any means, including photocopying, recording, or other electronic or mechanical methods, without the prior written permission of the publisher, except in the case of brief quotations embodied in critical reviews and certain other noncommercial uses permitted by copyright law. For permission requests, write to the publisher, addressed "Attention: Permissions Coordinator," at the address below.

Blue Beaver Publishing LLC
251-21 Jericho Turnpike
Bellerose NY 11426
www.bluebeaverpublishing.com

Printed in the United States of America
ISBN: 978-0-578-33396-0 (Paperback)

WELCOME

This is an invitation to embrace your wellbeing, create time and space for yourself, develop more self compassion, incorporate more joy into your life, and master the habit of prioritizing your self care. By purchasing this workbook, you've already taken the first step in prioritizing YOU!

To live a more mindful life requires space to be intentional, to curate a lifestyle that's supportive of your wellbeing. This workbook will guide you on how to do just that.

Allow yourself to be creative here, so set the mood, play your favorite songs, get colored pens or pencils and let's begin!

Rose

Commitment to Myself

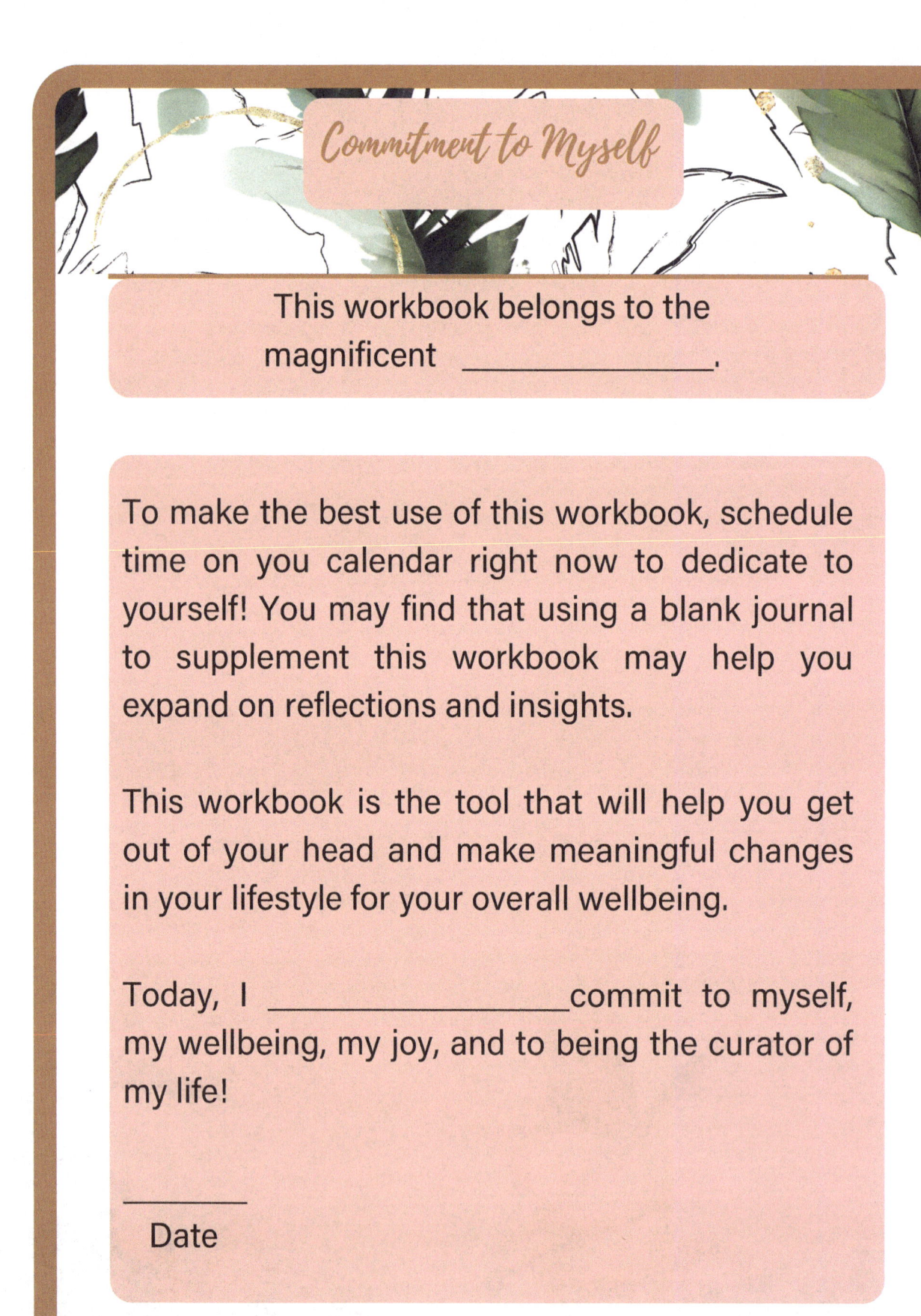

This workbook belongs to the magnificent _____.

To make the best use of this workbook, schedule time on you calendar right now to dedicate to yourself! You may find that using a blank journal to supplement this workbook may help you expand on reflections and insights.

This workbook is the tool that will help you get out of your head and make meaningful changes in your lifestyle for your overall wellbeing.

Today, I _____ commit to myself, my wellbeing, my joy, and to being the curator of my life!

_____
Date

Permission Slip

You're ALLOWED to enjoy the life you worked so hard to earn. You're ALLOWED to have your OWN goals and desires.

I _____, have permission to end the cycle of struggle and take the necessary steps to shift into a lifestyle that fulfills ME!

_____
Signature   Date

You're Worthy!

Your wellbeing is finally worthy of your attention!

Culture and society have pushed us to strive for success as the unit of measure of life achievement. For melanated women, an added layer of conforming and struggle have been forced upon us. You've been programmed to believe that your worth is only tied to your career, how productive you are, how well you fulfill your roles in life, and by the amount of material possessions you own.

As a result, you've become driven by outward validation for how many degrees you've earned, how much more money you can make, how perfect a daughter, mother, sister, friend, girlfriend, or wife you can be.

You're Worthy!

However, you're worth comes from being so much more than what you do!

This conditioning has minimized the value of your personal journey and your life experiences that have shaped you into the person you are today. Your personal experiences have allowed you to gain inner wisdom, which is something no educational institute or textbook could ever teach. This conditioning has also blurred your ability to see your true inherent worth, just as you are!

You're magnificent just for being YOU!

About Me

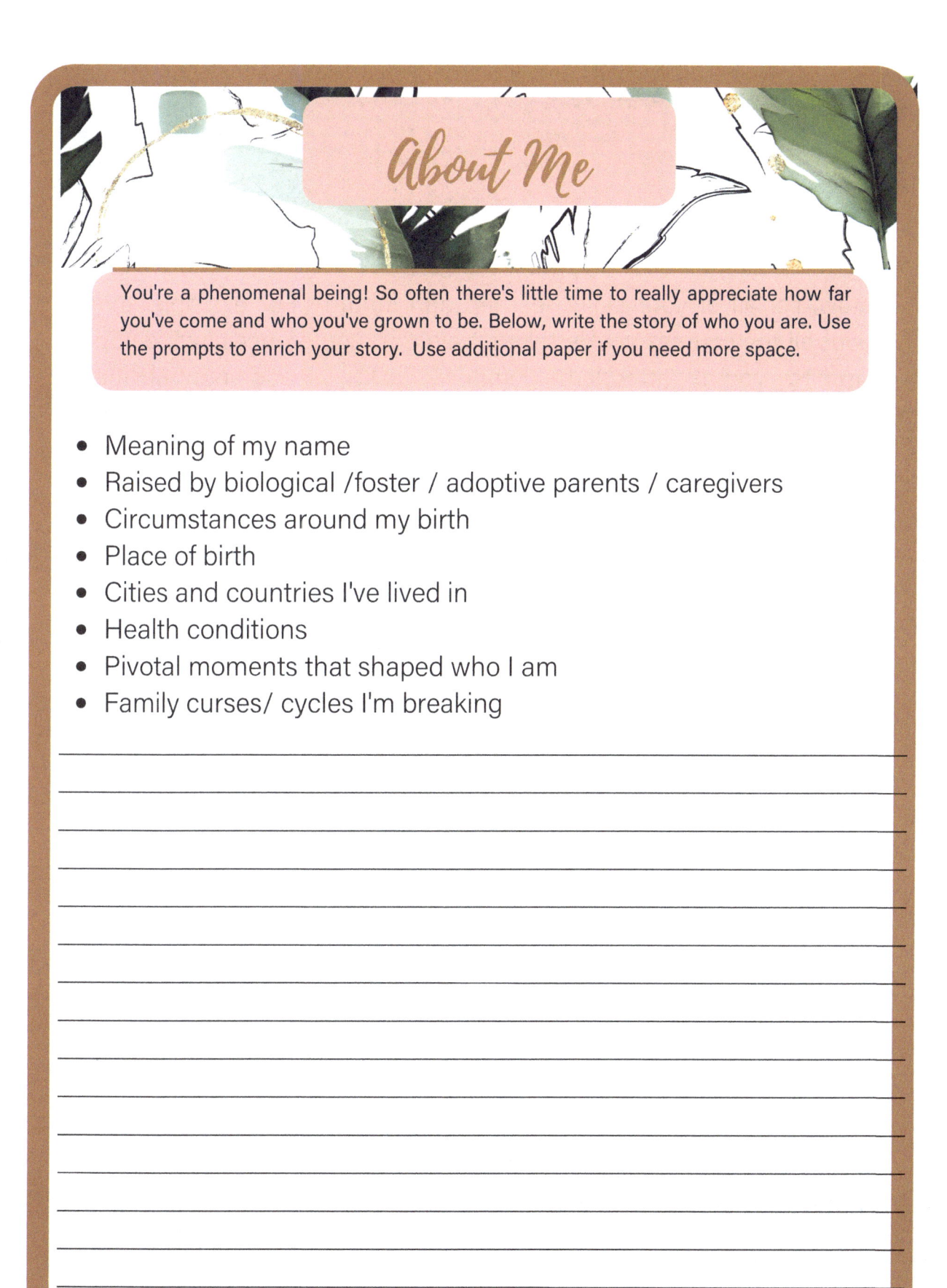

You're a phenomenal being! So often there's little time to really appreciate how far you've come and who you've grown to be. Below, write the story of who you are. Use the prompts to enrich your story. Use additional paper if you need more space.

- Meaning of my name
- Raised by biological /foster / adoptive parents / caregivers
- Circumstances around my birth
- Place of birth
- Cities and countries I've lived in
- Health conditions
- Pivotal moments that shaped who I am
- Family curses/ cycles I'm breaking

My Skills

Below, list all of your skills, learned and innate. For example, think about all the courses you've taken, trainings, conferences, workshops, summits you've attended, computer skills, leadership abilities, speaking engagements, home management, and life skills. This may take time to complete, so revisit this page and add information as it comes to you. Use additional paper if you need more space.

By the age of 21, I had learned _____
_____
_____

By the age of 28, I had learned
_____
_____
_____

By the age of 36, I had learned
_____
_____
_____

By the age of 42, I had learned
_____
_____
_____

By the age of 49, I had learned
_____
_____
_____

My Skills

Evaluate your skills by answering the following questions:

What's my learning style? Do I learn best by seeing, listening, doing, or writing?

Do I do my best work when I'm alone or with people?

What abilities and skills do I want to develop in myself?

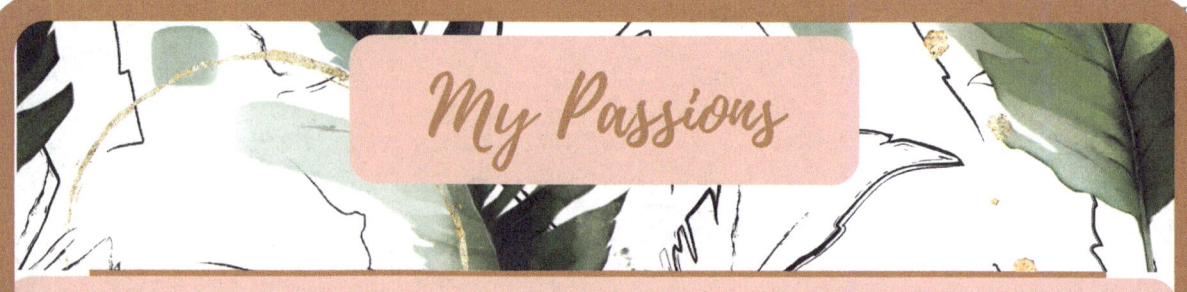

My Passions

Below, list your passions, hobbies, and interests throughout your life. What do you love to do for fun? What do you enJOY doing? Don't worry about how "good" you are at doing them. List them even if you were discouraged or just stopped doing them. This may take time to complete, so don't worry. Revisit this page, and add information as it comes to you.

My passions, hobbies, and interests:

By the age of 7 , I was always _____
_____
_____

By the age of 14, I was always _____
_____
_____

By the age of 21, I was always _____
_____
_____

By the age of 28, I was always _____
_____
_____

By the age of 36, I was always _____
_____
_____

Innate Gift(s)

We each have a unique gift, whether you're consciously aware of it or not. What is your unique gift? Is there a gift you have that you may be scared to share, or were discouraged from sharing? Our gifts are meant to be discovered and used to help others. In the circle below, write down what you think your gift is. You may have more than one.

Innate Gift(s)

Gratitude

Life has a way of making us focus on our problems or what's wrong. However, we also have many things that are going well for us! Using colored pen or pencils, starting from the circle outward, write all the things, people, and experiences that you are grateful for!

Example: I am grateful for having a place to live.

Example: I am grateful for my health.

I am grateful for

Most importantly, be sure to add yourself!

Love Letter

Now that you've written about your unique characteristics, take a moment to applaud yourself and be proud of who you are! For many Melanated Women, we were not raised on compliments, and we then find ourselves as adults having difficulty receiving them. However, receiving compliments is necessary to having a healthy sense of self. You can only receive what you feel you deserve.

Below, you will write yourself a love letter. Consider all of your personality traits, and characteristics. If this is difficult to do, ask close friends and family members what they love the most about you and incorporate that into your letter. Use your favorite color ink to write.

Example
Dear Rose,
You're compassionate, kind and have a heart of gold! You're creative, fun to be around, and I enjoy your spirit! Despite what you've been through, you've kept your inner joy!
Keep being you! I love you!
Always and Forever,
Me

My Purpose

Are you living in autopilot or in your purpose? Finding your purpose is an ever evolving journey. Most people do not have the time to even think about what their purpose is! But making the time to consider your purpose is a great first step.

Use this worksheet as a tool to start brainstorming what your purpose could be. Consider what you listed in the previous pages. Think about interests you had as a child, before life interfered and made you forget. Is there something you feel called to do? Is there a common thread between your passions and what people who know you well compliment you the most about? Is there an adversity you've overcome that might inspire or help others? In the circle below, write what your purpose could be.

My Purpose

Self Portrait

INTENTIONALLY LEFT BLANK

Self Portrait

You're a phenomenal being! You probably do not give yourself enough credit. Use the space below to create your self portrait. Find a favorite picture of you; one with you in bliss! Next, draw and write characteristics describing your favorite attributes. Frame this! If you want to be more creative, make a larger scale version by using poster board and put it in a visible place in your home.

My Self-Care

Self-Care Quiz

There's no judgement here. Simply answer honestly to get a baseline of your current self-care habits.
Score
- 2 points for each 'Yes'
- 1 point for each 'S / Sometimes'
- 0 point for 'No'

		Yes	S	No
1.	On average, I sleep well and feel rested	☐	☐	☐
2.	I am up-to-date with my health check-ups	☐	☐	☐
3.	I have time in my schedule for my hobbies	☐	☐	☐
4.	I eat healthy meals most of the time	☐	☐	☐
5.	I work within my mental and physical capacity	☐	☐	☐
6.	I set time for myself with a morning and bedtime routine	☐	☐	☐
7.	My lifestyle fulfills me	☐	☐	☐
8.	I practice effective stress management habits	☐	☐	☐

Your total score _____

What thoughts came up for you about your answers?

© 2021 Rose-Stella Pierre-Louis
www.RoseStella.com

Stress Management

Modern living is stressful. The work hours are extensive, the demands of life, obligations and responsibilities of being an adult are overwhelming, especially when you don't have adequate social, financial, or community support. Collectively, this takes a toll on our minds and bodies. For Melanated Women, we also experience the negative health impact of systemic racism, unresolved intergenerational trauma, migration-related trauma, impact of epigenetics, and adverse childhood experiences.

Prioritizing and taking care of your wellbeing is not a luxury, it's a necessity.

Our brain and body's primary function is to keep us safe and alive. They do this by continuously communicating with each other, keeping a pulse on the various interconnected systems within our bodies, while also taking in information about our environment. Our bodies were designed for occasional stress, however chronic stress causes severe health impairments.

Our bodies perceive stress as danger. Your brain cannot tell the difference between an immediate threat (e.g. danger from an oncoming car), or stress (e.g. fear of getting to work late).

When your life become a series of moments of stress, (e.g. running late, not meeting a work deadline) **your brain and body function in survival mode.**

Your brain in turn floods your body with stress hormones (cortisol & adrenaline). Being in this prolonged state contributes to chronic diseases.

That's why it is crucial to take care of your mental and physical wellbeing daily.

Stress Responses

While we can't control the stressors and real dangers in our environments, we can control our stress levels. There are habits that no longer serve you. While they may have enabled you to succeed at school and in your career, and were necessary for our family's survival, they negatively impact your wellbeing.

Working under pressure, perfectionism, superwoman syndrome, and being the model minority may appear to be admirable work ethics, but they contribute to your stress levels. Working to exhaustion to meet high demands and unreasonable expectations, cause stress responses in our brains and bodies.

Stress responses are your body's signal to communicate with you that functioning past it's normal capacity.

Stress Responses

Stress response symptoms may appear as the following:

- tightness in neck or jaw
- difficulty taking deep relaxing breaths
- stomachaches
- loose stool or constipation
- back aches
- chronic fatigue
- painful / heavy / irregular periods
- yeast infections
- difficulty sleeping

Your Stress Responses

Sometimes we've experienced stress response symptoms for so long they've become normal. Take the time now to give your body the attention it deserves. Going from head to toe, think about the signals you may have ignored. Use the picture on the previous page to circle body parts that may require tender loving care.

What signals has your body been sending you that you've minimized?

Is there reoccurring pain or discomfort you find yourself taking care of frequently? (e.g. medicine for migraines or irritable stomach)

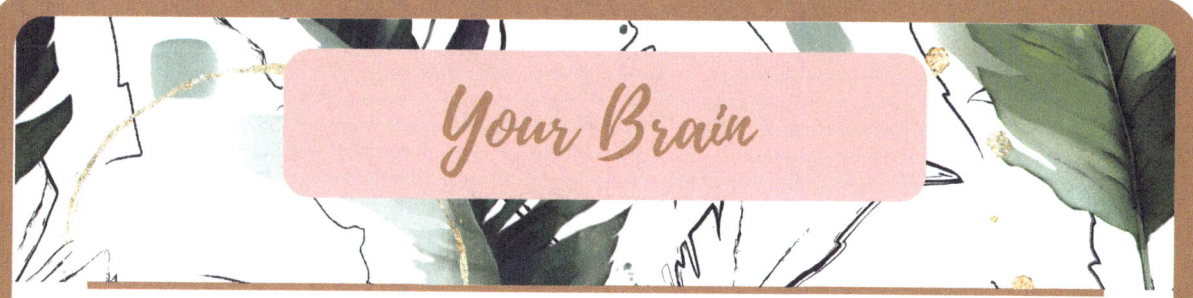

Your Brain

We are our toughest critics. Often, we silently beat ourselves up with a critical inner dialogue.

Your habits are driven by the inner dialogue in your mind. The inner dialogue is a combination of repeated messages you've internalized, beliefs you inherited from your upbringing, behaviors you modeled, as well as from your personal experiences. These messages and beliefs make up your subconscious mind. Dealing with your inner critic and changing your beliefs aren't things you can just will yourself to do, so don't be so hard on yourself. It takes time, intention, and learning how to work with your brain.

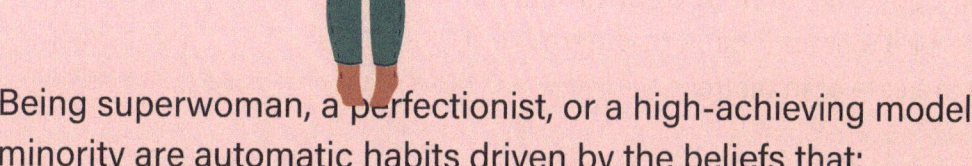

Being superwoman, a perfectionist, or a high-achieving model minority are automatic habits driven by the beliefs that:
- *I have to be a strong Black woman no matter what*
- *I have to give 110% to show my worth*
- *I have to keep my emotions under control*
- *No one can do it like I can, so I'll just do it myself everytime*
- *I'm a failure if I'm not perfect*

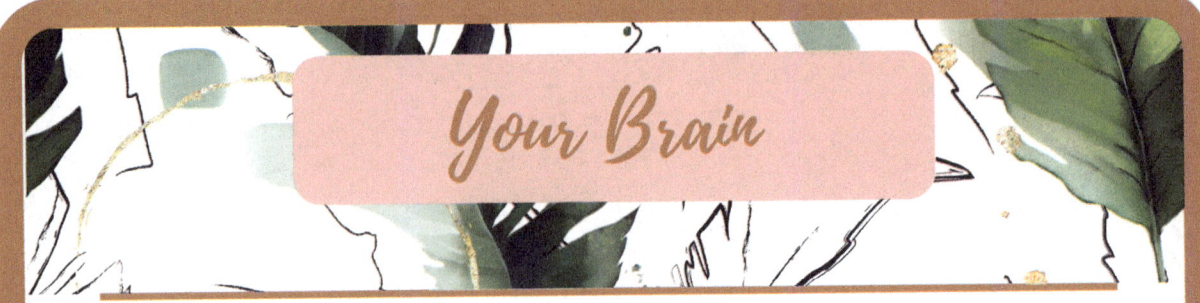

Your Brain

Your brain is a complex organ, so for the purpose of this workbook, we will only focus on three parts of it. They are responsible for how you manage stress and where your beliefs exist.

Your thinking brain, the pre-frontal cortex, is responsible for advanced functions like critical thinking, learning, planning, and making decisions.

Your emotional brain, the limbic system, houses your beliefs, and processes your memories and feelings.

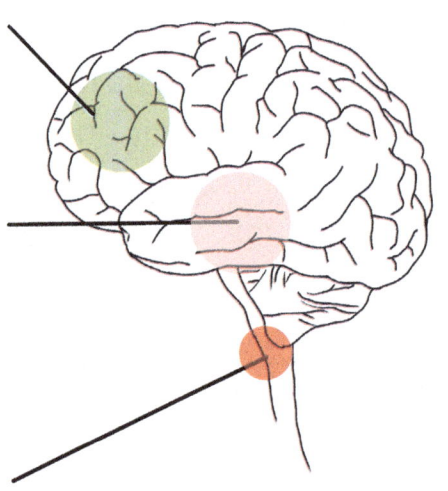

Your survival brain, the brainstem, is the headquarters of your brain. It filters every experience and signal from within your body and from your environment. One of it's main jobs is to determine if you are safe or in distress.

When you're safe, it allows all your inner systems to function as usual and your thinking brain is in control. However, when you're stressed, your survival brain takes over, and shuts down communication with your thinking brain. Once in this state, you function in a reactionary state that's purely reflexive. This reactionary state is referred to as fight, flight, freeze, or fawn stress response.

Stress Responses

FIGHT RESPONSES
- Argumentative
- Controlling
- Ultra-independent

FLIGHT RESPONSES
- Over-worry
- Workaholic

FREEZE RESPONSES
- Indecisive
- Spaces out

FAWN RESPONSES
- People please
- Difficulty saying no

This is a simple diagram showing the four stress responses and some behaviors they show up. What many people think are personality traits or behaviors, are actually stress responses. Stress responses are more dynamic, however for the purpose of this workbook, they are described for a general understanding.

Your Brain

Your brain has the most powerful influence on your wellbeing. The beliefs in your emotional brain can either calm you or trigger your brain to signal stress responses in your body. It's up to you to decide. It is within your control to chose what beliefs you want to focus on and to chose environments (when possible) with reduced levels of stress.

Thanks to neuroplasticity, your brain is flexible, so you can change your beliefs and stress responses, no matter your age or circumstance.

You can intentionally create new beliefs, habits, and inner dialogue!

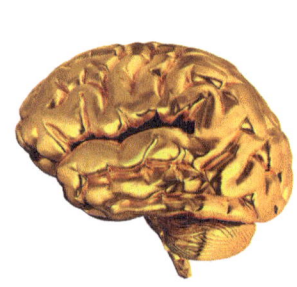

Inherited Beliefs

Circle the beliefs you've internalized:

Race
- *Natural course, curly, kinky hair is ugly and unprofessional.*
- *Darker skin is less desirable than lighter skin.*

Gender roles
- *A woman's body should be "in shape" to attract a male partner.*
- *Beauty is wearing make up and dressing "well".*
- *Men are superior to women.*
- *All women want to bear children and are natural nurturers.*
- *A good woman takes care of her family.*
- *Women should take time off to take are of their children.*
- *Primary job is taking care of family and secondary job is working.*
- *Only heterosexual relationships are "acceptable".*
- *Women are responsible for all household chores, including cooking, cleaning, and laundering clothes, and making meals for the family.*
- *A woman's life goals are to get married and have children.*
- *It's important to be good and put others needs before your own.*

Cultural roles
- *It's important that other people have a good impression of you.*
- *Asking for help is a sign of weakness.*
- *You have to stay strong and keep it together under all circumstance.*
- *Therapy is for crazy people. It's a place to air out your family's "dirty laundry".*
- *Work is more important than socializing or family life.*
- *Success and happiness are having a career, getting married, and having children.*
- *Your worth depends on how many degrees, awards, and certifications you've earned.*
- *Work hard in one career and work until retirement.*
- *You stick by your family no matter how bad they treat you.*
- *Providing basic needs, like food and shelter, is more important than caring for emotional needs, such as love, care, and affection.*

My Inherited Beliefs

In what ways do these beliefs impact how you show up for

yourself?

your family?

in friendships?

in your relationships (personal and professional)?

in your career?

Which beliefs are you willing to challenge and change?

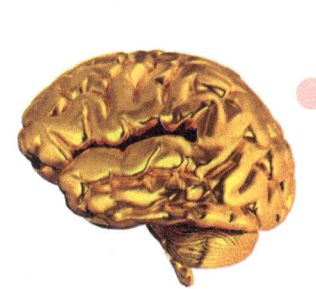

New Beliefs

- I prioritize my health and wellbeing.
- Experiencing my feelings is healthy.
- I am a human being so I am perfectly imperfect.
- I am a human BEing, not a human DOing.
- My natural hair is beautiful.
- My skin protects me and is beautiful.
- Men and women can contribute to caring for a family.
- I can have more than 1 career in life.
- Asking for help is empowering.
- It's important for me to be my authentic self.

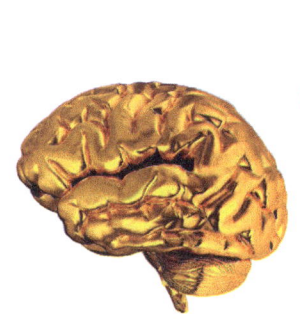

My New Beliefs

List beliefs you want to live by:

Stress Response Reflections

With this new awareness of the relationship between your brain and your stress responses, what thoughts or insights come up for you?

_____
_____
_____
_____
_____
_____

What are ways you can honor your mind and body and address these signals?

_____
_____
_____
_____
_____
_____
_____
_____

What are ways you can be kind with your thoughts, and gentler with yourself?

_____
_____
_____
_____
_____
_____
_____
_____

Healthy Habits

Below are some examples of healthy habits that reduce the stress responses in your body.
I honor my body by

- Creating morning and bedtime routine with intention, where I am disconnected from social media and spend dedicated time with myself
- I will schedule regular quiet time for myself to pray or meditate
- Enforce my boundaries so that I don't overwork myself
- Make more time to spend with my family and friends
- Be intentional when eating meals eating undistracted

My Healthy Habits

List ways you honor your body and add additional ways.
I honor my body by _____

_____
_____
_____
_____
_____
_____
_____
_____
_____
_____
_____

My Specialists

You may need additional support from a specialist or professional to address your stress responses. You may also benefit from working with professionals who specialize in the health and wellbeing of Melanated Women. Not all therapists and healers are alike. Be sure to choose someone who is culturally sensitive, and who specializes in your specific stress responses.

Keep in mind, we come from a lineage and ancestry who've practiced holistic medicine for centuries before the development of modern western medicine.

Consider searching for a:
- somatic therapist
- trauma informed therapist
- spiritual healer
- energy healer
- shaman

Current Self Care

It takes time and practice to learn how to prioritize yourself and how to incorporate self-care regularly. Below, taking inventory of what your current self-care routine looks like.

Daily

Weekly

Monthly

Types of Self Care

You are most likely still learning to prioritize self-care in your life. Self-care is usually thought of as taking care of physical needs, like pampering yourself with a manicure, taking a break from work, or getting a massage. But SELF-care includes all aspects of yourSELF.

Deeper Dive
Mental Wellbeing

Taking care of your mental wellbeing is just as important as taking care of your physical wellbeing. While taking care of your physical wellbeing is easier to measure because you can see the results immediately (e.g. use a scale to track weight loss, time how long you've done a work out, admire the shine of your manicure), tracking your mental wellbeing requires you to pay close attention to your inner state. The unit of measure of your state of mental wellbeing includes feeling at ease, having peace of mind, and having encouraging inner dialogue.

As mentioned earlier, your mental wellbeing is influenced by your inner beliefs and the messages you internalize from your environment.

What I Feed My Mind

This week, track who your interact with and the type of social media you expose yourself to regularly.

How do you feel after being with certain people? Do you feel energized or depleted?

How much time do you spend on tv and social media and what type of content do you spend most of your time watching?

How do you feel after watching tv or being on social media? Encouraged, inspired, anxious, or frustrated?

Who and what environments support integrating healthy self-care habits into your life?

Types of Self Care

Physical
Taking care of the needs of your beautiful body. This includes movement, and what you put in and on your body (e.g. exercise, food, medicine, hair and body products).

Emotional
Being in tune with your emotions and how you regulate them. This includes how you manage your daily stresses.

Mental
Keeping your creative juices flowing, having joy, and passion in your life by engaging in meaningful work and hobbies.

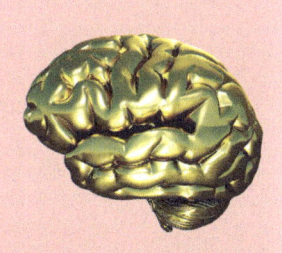

Spiritual
Ways in which you stay connected to a high power greater than yourself. The ways you stay aligned with your soul and purpose.

Types of Self Care
Examples

Physical
Workout class Mondays & Wednesdays
Meal prep on Sundays to cook healthy meals and snacks for the week.

Emotional
Journal every night.
Session with therapist every week.

Mental
Dance class on Saturday.
Art class Tuesday night.

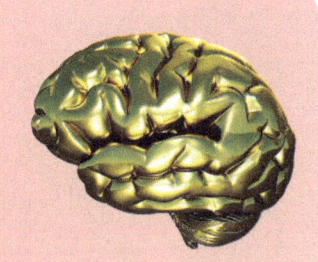

Spiritual
Meditate or pray in the morning and right before bed.

Your Self Care Menu

List the types of self-care you currently use and add new ones you will incorporate into your routine.

Physical
(e.g. sleep, water intake, food, & exercise)

Emotional
(e.g. journaling, therapy, identifying triggers, setting boundaries.)

Mental
(e.g. hobbies, learning.)

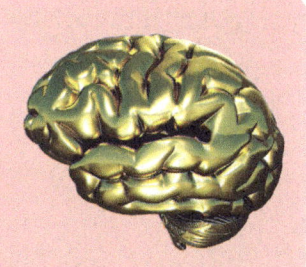

Spiritual
(e.g. prayer, meditation, nature.)

Daily Self Care

Write new self-care practices you will add to your routines.

Morning Routine

Bedtime Routine

(Note: Disconnecting from electronics 1 hour before sleep helps regulate your sleep cycle.

Self Care Routine

Self Care Weekly Planner

Month:

Week:

Write new weekly self-care practices you will add to your routines.

Monday

Tuesday

Wednesday

Thursday

Friday

Saturday

Sunday

Notes:

My Lifestyle

Current Lifestyle

To make the shift from overdoing to prioritizing your wellbeing, requires you to explore aspects of your lifestyle that are supportive of your wellbeing and those that negatively impact it.

Is your lifestyle supportive of your wellbeing?

Does it fulfill you?

Current Lifestyle

Taking inventory of how you spend your time, allows you to see where your focus and energy are used the most. Using colored pen or pencil, divide the circle into how your time is currently spent in all areas of your life.

Current Lifestyle

Review the circle, then answer the following questions.

What thoughts and insights came up for you?
_____
_____
_____
_____

Which areas fill your cup and which drain you?
_____
_____
_____

Does this current lifestyle fulfill and satisfy you? Why or why not?
_____
_____
_____
_____

What areas would you like to see changed and why?
_____
_____
_____
_____
_____
_____

Ideal Lifestyle

In a quiet space, close your eyes and envision the ideal life you want for yourself. Using colored pen or pencil, divide the circle into how you'd ideally want your time to be spent.

Insights

Once you've completed the diagram on your ideal lifestyle, what thoughts or insights came up for you?

_____
_____
_____
_____
_____
_____
_____
_____
_____
_____
_____
_____
_____
_____
_____
_____
_____

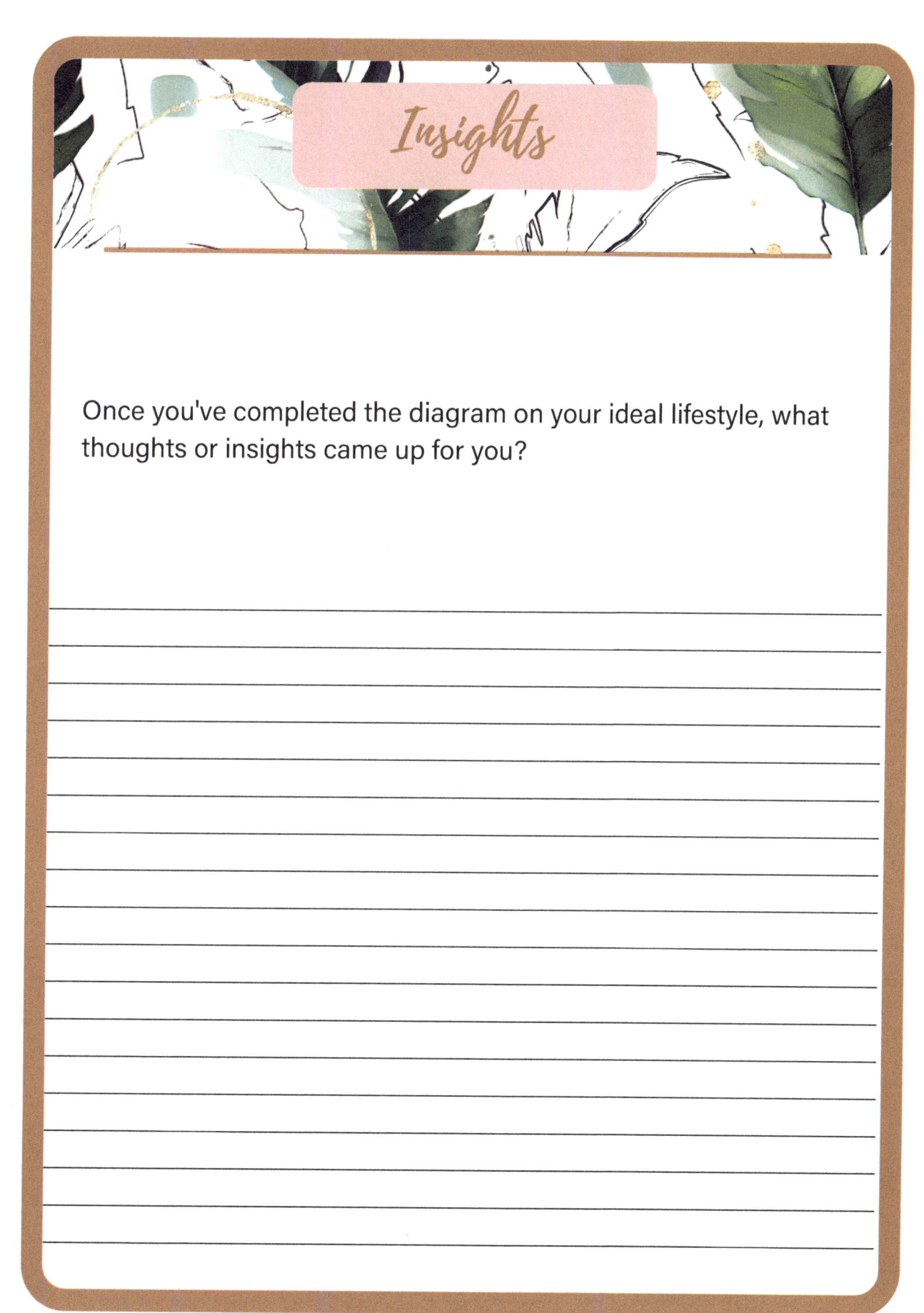

Stellar Shift Action Plan

Use the space below to brainstorm how to shift from your current lifestyle to your ideal lifestyle. The time and effort you spend here is powerful because it is the first step in bridging the gap. Use additional paper if needed.

What habits would you keep?

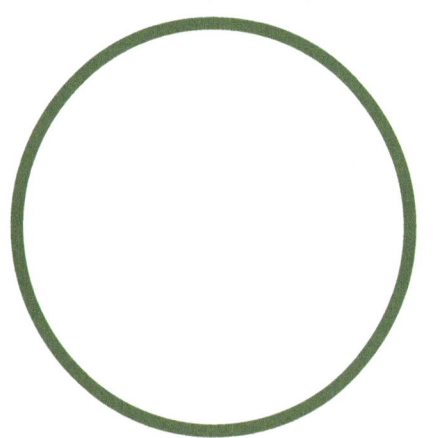

What habits would you have to change?

What skills would you need to use or learn?

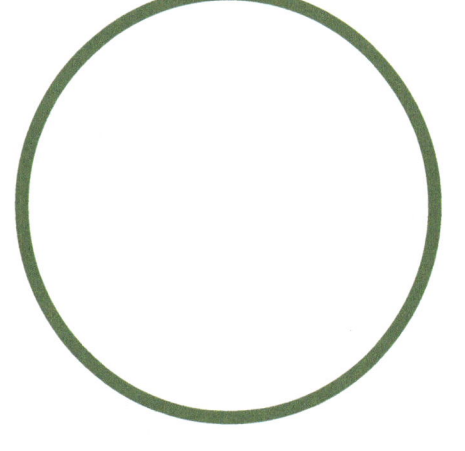

What obligations can you delegate or give up all together from your current life?

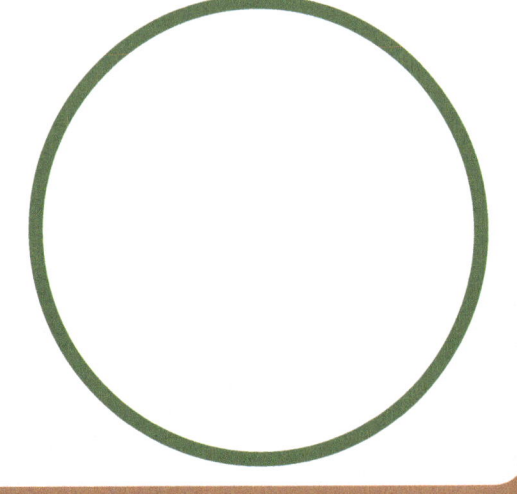

My Goals

Goals!

Write down your goals to make long lasting changes in your life and achieve your dreams.

We all have dreams for ourselves. Many of us don't entertain the real possibility for our dreams to come true because they seem so far out of reach. In actuality, you can reach your dreams by creating small, achievable goals, that collectively get you closer to realizing your dreams.

Goals help organize your responsibilities and prioritize your time. They give direction and guide your personal development journey. The best way to make long lasting changes in your life is to set and write down your goals.

Writing down your goals, transforms them from ideas in your head to tangible, real life tasks. Study after study show that most people don't stick to their goals because they don't write them down! And of the ones who do write them down, they don't keep their goals in a visible place to reference daily.

By being intentional and taking the time to write your goals, you're taking the steps to ensure you achieve your goals and dreams!

Obstacles

Another practice to ensure that you will achieve success, is to identify barriers that have prevented or continue to prevent you from achieving your goals. List all the reasons you can think of. Consider the following; friends, family members, circumstances, life events, work, lack of resources, money, etc.

Stepping Stones

Identify the supports you will need to overcome the obstacles listed. The two most important supports, or stepping stones, to achieve your goals are your inner beliefs and your environment. Write down people, spaces, supplies, etc. that will support you.

FEARS

Fears always come up when you stretch yourself out of your comfort zone to grow, make changes in your life, and achieve new goals. The great thing about this is that fears can be overcome! So be brave, and list ALL THE FEARS and messages your inner critic is saying around trying to achieve your goals.

Overcoming Fears

Now that you've listed your fears, you've taken the first step in taking their power away! Writing fears down gives you the opportunity to shed light, truly examine how true they are, and gives you the opportunity to stop them from holding you back! Go back to the previous sheet, and cross out each fear and rewrite a new truth. Using colored pen or pencil, list the new truths below.

Life Fulfillment

1. Review the life areas.
2. Write a number between 1 (very dissatisfied) and 10 (satisfied) for each category. Write the FIRST number that comes to mind, not the number you think it should be.
3. Color and fill in each area, with the center of the wheel being 0 and the outer edge being 10.

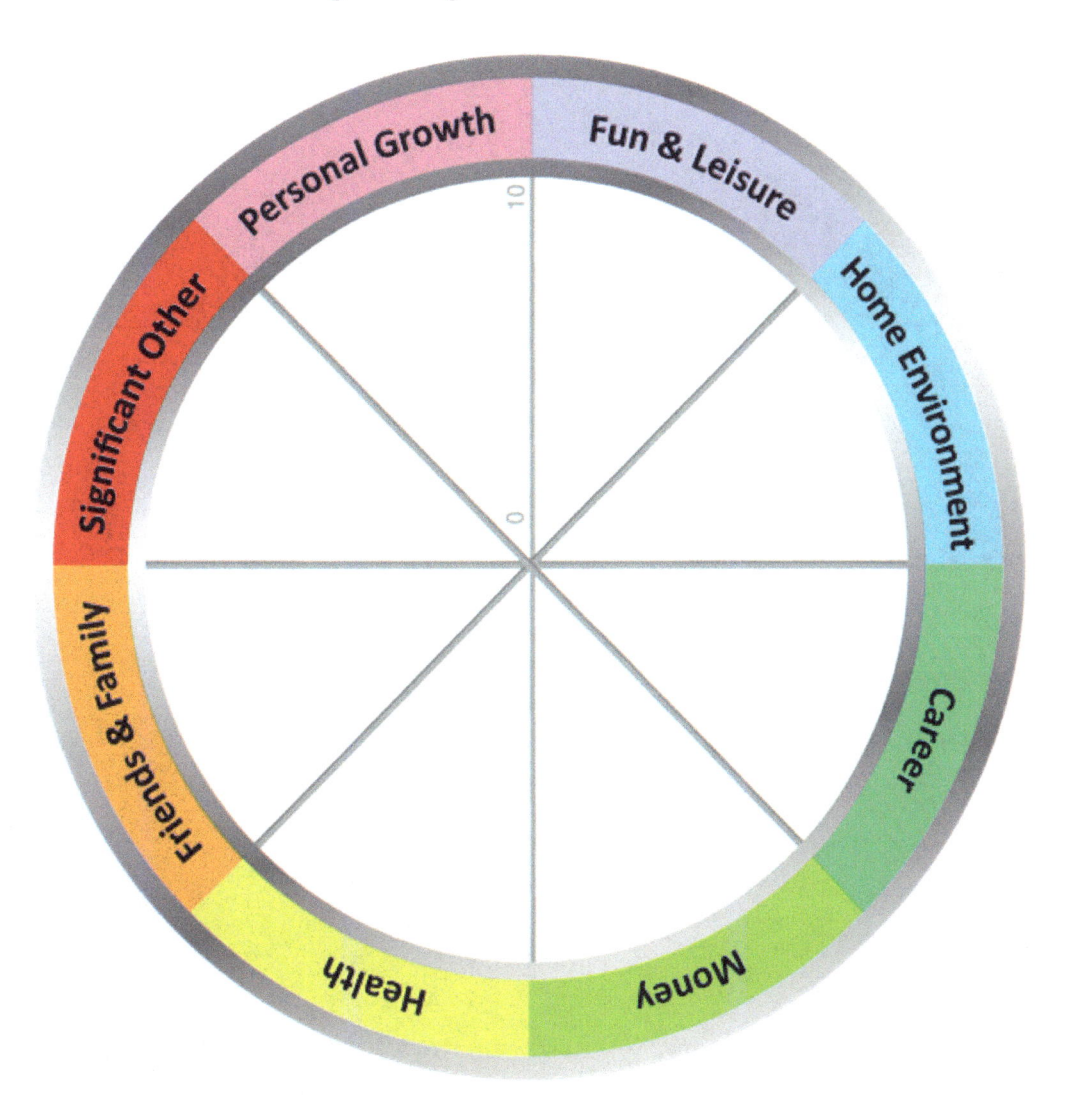

Ideal Life Fulfillment

1. Review the life areas.
2. Write a number you WANT for each life area, 1 (very dissatisfied) and 10 (satisfied).
3. Color and fill in each area, with the center of the wheel being 0 and the outer edge being 10.

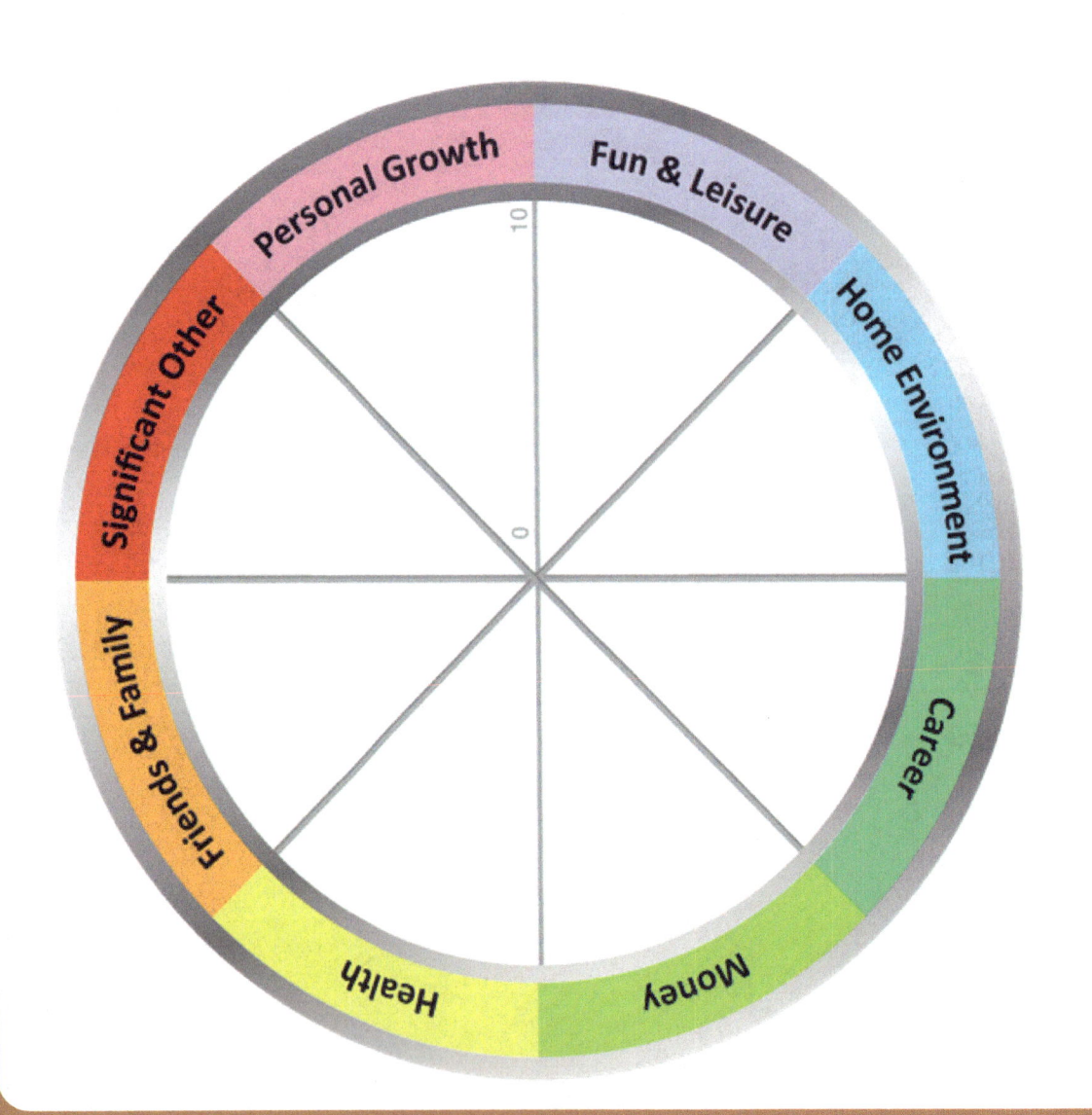

Wheel segments: Personal Growth, Fun & Leisure, Home Environment, Career, Money, Health, Friends & Family, Significant Other

Goal Writing

In the next section you will write your goals. Although there are eight life areas to chose from, focus on 1-2 areas, and only write 1 goal for each.

When choosing a goal, refer back to the skills, passions, and purpose worksheets in the About Me section, as well as your self-care menu, and specialists, in the My Self-Care section. Be sure to include goals around these.

On the worksheets titled Baseline, write what your life currently looks like in that area. On the My Goals worksheets, select 1-2 life areas, and write a goal you want to achieve based on your baseline.

The most common mistakes in setting goals are
- not breaking them down to achievable steps
- not making them measurable
- and tackling too many goals at once.

An effective method for writing goals is using the S.M.A.R.T. method. It's an acronym that stands for:

Specific - What will I do?
Measurable - How will I do it?
Attainable - Is it achievable?
Relevant - Why will I do it?
Time frame - When will I do it?

Once you've achieved those goals, come back and work on 1 - 2 additional goals.

Goal Writing

Here are some examples of S.M.A.R.T. goals:

Life area: Fun and leisure
Baseline: I don't have time for any hobbies.
Goal: I will attend an art class 1 night a week by October.
S - attend art class
M - 1 night a week
A - I don't participate in any hobbies because I work so much
R - to improve my work - life balance
T - by October

Life area: Personal Growth
Baseline: I read self-help books but don't implement what I've learned.
Goal: I will take 30 minutes a day to disconnect from social media to say positive affirmations and journal, by April.
S - journal + say positive affirmation
M - 30 minutes a day
A - I'm on social media all the time
R - reduce addiction to social media
T - by April

Life area: Health
Baseline: I work out every once in a while or when I feel like it.
Goal: I will work out for 20 minutes, 3 days a week in 12 weeks, either by walking or going to an exercise class.
S - work out
M - 20 minutes, 3 days a week
A - I currently get exhausted after working out for 5 mins!
R - lose weight, long term health, and stress management
T - in 12 weeks

© 2021 Rose-Stella Pierre-Louis
www.RoseStella.com

My Baseline

Personal Growth

Health

Fun & Leisure

Home

My Baseline

Friends & Family

Significant Other

Money

Career

My Goals

Personal Growth

Health

Fun & Leisure

Home

My Goals

Friends & Family

Significant Other

Money

Career

My Action Plan

Wonderful! You've taken the first steps to achieve your goals!

Next step is to schedule dedicated recurring appointments on your calendar to work on your goal(s). COMMIT TO THEM! (Refer back to your signature on page 2.)

Indicate the deadline, the days of the week, and how much time per day you'll need to commit.

Schedule time to purchase supplies, schedule a service, or contact the people who will help you achieve your goal(s). Reference back to the list of all the supports you will need.

Add stickers, draw balloons, stars, or schedule a special dinner to celebrate your goal date.

To continue to set yourself for success, be realistic and compassionate with yourself. There will be days when your scheduled gets derailed, you're exhausted, or something unexpected happens. Be easy on your self, and continue when humanly possible.

I'm rooting for you and have faith in your success!

Goals Weekly Planner

Month:

Week:

Write the goal(s) you will commit to working on.

Monday

Tuesday

Wednesday

Thursday

Friday

Saturday

Sunday

Notes:

Year At Glance

Write the goals you will work to achieve in the months below.

JANUARY	FEBRUARY	MARCH

APRIL	MAY	JUNE

JULY	AUGUST	SEPTEMBER

OCTOBER	NOVEMBER	DECEMBER

My Supreme Dreams

I want you to wonder outside the boundaries of what you think is possible for you. Think big! What dreams and desires are so magnificent you can't even conceive how they can happen? Write or draw them below, sign, date and revisit this sheet in one year.

You did it!

You've accepted this invitation and committed to yourself! You've made the time to be intentional about your wellbeing and your life. You allowed yourself to explore who you are outside of the boundaries of generational cycles, struggle narrative, labels, and roles.

Hopefully you've developed a softer, more intimate, and kinder relationship with yourself. Feel free to share your insights, wins, and achievements on my social media sites!

Keep going and growing!

Much Love & Encouragement,

Rose

Want more personalized guidance?

Join Our Coaching Program!

In this unique 8-week program, designed specifically for busy melanated women, you'll:

- Implement a comprehensive self-care routine into your busy schedule.

- Create your Self-Discovery Plan; the blueprint for discovering your gifts and purpose.

- Receive subconscious re-programming messages to overcome imposter syndrome.

- Identify your stress responses to end overworking to exhaustion.

- Discover and release limiting beliefs and habits that keep you stuck in the stress cycle.

REGISTER BY VISITING
www.RoseStella.com

About The Author

Rose-Stella Pierre-Louis is a multi-lingual Haitian-American transformation coach for first-generation women and the founder of Stellar Transformation, LLC. Her exclusive signature coaching program offers a creative, unique and compassionate approach to support women in reprogramming cultural limiting beliefs so they can shift to a lifestyle that offers long-lasting peace of mind, joy, and ease.

Rose-Stella is passionate about helping women prioritize their well-being after meeting their cultural and family obligations. She has navigated the weight of expectations on first-generation women including being a high-achieving professional and experiencing burnout, motherhood, marriage, divorce, and end-of-life planning for parents, and now helps guide women through a similar journey with less stress.

Rose-Stella was a keynote speaker at the Redwood Empire Chapter of the California Association for the Education of Young Children, speaker at California Forum for Professional Development conferences and has guest-lectured at Sacramento State University and Los Rios Community College on human development, regulating the stressed nervous system, and using brain-body synching methods to break hard habits.

Rose-Stella is also an Occupational Therapist OTR/L (14 years) with a private practice, Ms. Rose's TheraPlace. She lives with her two children in Sacramento, CA where she enjoys the bliss of playing, dancing, sunbathing, and laughing.

© 2021 Stellar Transformation LLC
www.RoseStellaPierreLouis.com

Made in the USA
Columbia, SC
21 December 2021